THE VIETNAM WAR
12 THINGS TO KNOW

by Jill Sherman

12 STORY LIBRARY

www.12StoryLibrary.com

12-Story Library is an imprint of Peterson Publishing Company and Press Room Editions.

Produced for 12-Story Library by Red Line Editorial

Photographs ©: AP Images, cover, 1, 13, 14, 16, 22, 28, 29; Bettmann/Corbis, 4, 6, 7, 12, 26; Thomas J. O'Halloran/Library of Congress, 9, 21, 23; US Department of Defense/AP Images, 10; Age Fotostock/Alamy, 11; xuanhuongho/iStockphoto, 17; Dennis Gray/AP Photo, 18; Warren K. Leffler/Library of Congress, 20; Public Domain, 25; James P. Blair/Corbis, 27

Content Consultant: Professor Robert F. Turner, Center for National Security Law, University of Virginia Law School

Library of Congress Cataloging-in-Publication Data
Names: Sherman, Jill, author.
Title: The Vietnam War : 12 things to know / by Jill Sherman.
Other titles: Vietnam War, twelve things to know
Description: Mankato, MN : 12-Story Library, [2017] | Series: America at war
  | Includes bibliographical references and index. | Audience: Grades 4-6.
Identifiers: LCCN 2016002425 (print) | LCCN 2016002587 (ebook) | ISBN
  9781632352675 (library bound : alk. paper) | ISBN 9781632353177 (pbk. :
  alk. paper) | ISBN 9781621434368 (hosted ebook)
Subjects: LCSH: Vietnam War, 1961-1975--Juvenile literature.
Classification: LCC DS557.7 .S497 2016 (print) | LCC DS557.7 (ebook) | DDC
  959.704/3--dc23
LC record available at http://lccn.loc.gov/2016002425

Printed in the United States of America
Mankato, MN
May, 2016

Access free, up-to-date content on this topic plus a full digital version of this book. Scan the QR code on page 31 or use your school's login at 12StoryLibrary.com.

Table of Contents

1

Nations Fight for Control of Indochina Colonies

World War II (1939–1945) left countries everywhere in tatters. The war's destruction was vast. France scraped through on the side of the Allies. But it had lost control of its colonies in Asia during the war. Known as French Indochina, these colonies included Vietnam, Laos, and Cambodia. After the war ended, France wasted no time trying to reclaim the colonies.

Many Vietnamese did not want to return to French colonial rule. Instead, on September 2, 1945, Vietnamese leader Ho Chi Minh declared Vietnam's independence. Ho was a communist. He wanted to see a revolution in Vietnam. He promised freedom, human rights, and democracy. His army, the Viet Minh, prepared for war. They wanted to remove the French from Vietnam. In 1946, this sparked the First Indochina War.

Though weakened by World War II, France had the aid of troops from southern Vietnam. In 1950, the United States threw its support behind France as well. US President Harry S. Truman wanted to help prevent the spread of communism. China had become a communist country in 1949. Truman did not want to see the same thing happen in Vietnam. He feared that if the

French soldier in Saigon

17th

Parallel line north of the equator at which Vietnam was divided in the Geneva Accords.

- France wanted to reclaim the colonies it lost during World War II.
- Ho Chi Minh declared Vietnam's independence and prepared for war.
- The First Indochina War lasted seven and a half years.
- Peace agreements were signed on July 20 and 21, 1954.

A LEADER FOR VIETNAM

Ho Chi Minh was born with the name Nguyen Tat Thanh on May 19, 1890. He left Vietnam in 1911 to seek work in France. He helped found the French Communist Party in 1920. Then he traveled to Moscow to study communism. When the Japanese took Vietnam in World War II, Ho returned home. He founded the Viet Minh to fight for independence. He also adopted a new name, Ho Chi Minh. It means "Bringer of Light."

Viet Minh won the war, it would pave the way for communism to spread throughout Asia.

With US guns and supplies, the French held control of the Vietnamese city of Saigon. But the Viet Minh were unwilling to accept defeat. Aided by Communist China, they assaulted the French troops. The war raged for years. In the spring of 1954, the Viet Minh held a siege on the French base at Dien Bien Phu. After 55 days, the French surrendered.

Peace agreements were signed on July 20 and 21, 1954. These international agreements were known as the Geneva Accords. One of them gave Vietnam two temporary governments. The Communist Democratic Republic of Vietnam controlled the North. The noncommunist Associated State of Vietnam controlled the South. The agreement also promised elections would be held in 1956. Government officials hoped these elections would once again unite Vietnam.

Ho Chi Minh Establishes a Communist Vietnam

Ho Chi Minh governed the northern part of Vietnam. It became a communist country. As president, Ho banned all noncommunist political parties. He also put in place many communist reforms. These were meant to create equality. Instead, they were used to treat people harshly.

The most notable was the land reform program. It started in 1953. The government took privately owned land. Then, it gave the land to peasants. Landlords were publicly shamed. They had their possessions taken from them. They were often forced to do menial jobs in labor camps. Many landlords were beaten and abused. Many of them were executed. Approximately 15,000 landowners were killed during the land reforms. A further 50,000 to 100,000 were deported or imprisoned.

Still, Ho hoped to unite Vietnam under his control. But the 1956

In 1930, Ho Chi Minh helped found the Indochinese Communist Party.

elections promised in the Geneva Accords never took place. Ngo Dinh Diem was the president of South Vietnam. He strongly opposed communism. He argued the Communists would never hold a fair election. Diem asked for the United Nations to supervise the elections to ensure they would be fair. But the Communists objected. With US support, Diem refused to take part in an unsupervised election.

That same year, Diem ended local elections in his own country. He suppressed his political rivals. And he became more and more unpopular. It did not take long for many South Vietnamese to start rebelling. They rose up against the government. Diem called them the Viet Cong. The name was short for "Viet Nam Cong San." In English, this means "Vietnamese Communists." But few rebels were part of the Communist Party. By the early 1960s, discontent was widespread. The Viet Cong threatened to topple Diem's government.

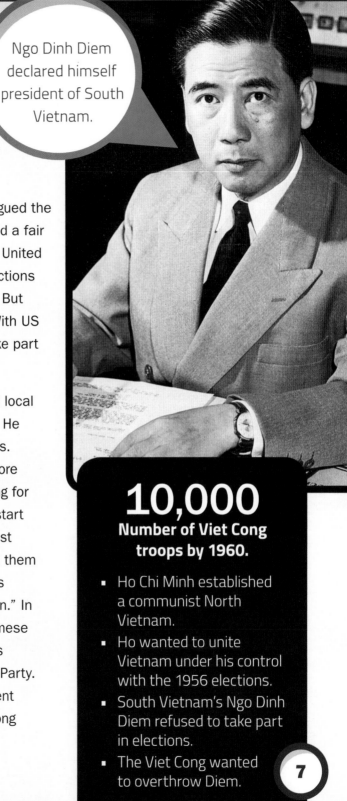

Ngo Dinh Diem declared himself president of South Vietnam.

10,000
Number of Viet Cong troops by 1960.

- Ho Chi Minh established a communist North Vietnam.
- Ho wanted to unite Vietnam under his control with the 1956 elections.
- South Vietnam's Ngo Dinh Diem refused to take part in elections.
- The Viet Cong wanted to overthrow Diem.

7

US Presidents Follow Truman Doctrine

US policy in Vietnam was based on President Harry S. Truman's Cold War policy. The Cold War (1945–1991) was a state of tension and mistrust between communist and noncommunist nations. Starting in 1947, under Truman, the United States provided aid to any nation threatened by communism. This policy was also known as the Truman Doctrine.

Following Truman's lead, presidents Dwight D. Eisenhower and John F. Kennedy also supported South Vietnam. They sent economic and military aid. In 1955, Eisenhower sent civilian and military advisers. They helped President Diem maintain control. Kennedy expanded US aid further. In 1962, he set up the Military Assistance Command, Vietnam (MACV). It provided US military advisers to train the South Vietnamese army. The US government claimed it had no military forces in

Vietnam, only advisers. But the number of military advisers under Kennedy rose from fewer than 1,000 to more than 15,000.

Lyndon B. Johnson became president after Kennedy was assassinated in 1963. Under Johnson, US involvement in Vietnam grew vastly. He did not want to go

46
Number of years the Cold War lasted.

- The Truman Doctrine was established on March 12, 1947, to aid countries threatened by communism.
- US presidents feared communism would spread throughout Asia.
- President Johnson increased US involvement and commitment to the war in Vietnam.

Lyndon B. Johnson on a visit to South Vietnam in 1961

to war. But he wanted to honor Kennedy's commitment to support South Vietnam. He planned to follow the Truman Doctrine to contain the spread of communism.

In early August 1964, Johnson received reports that two US destroyers had been attacked by the North Vietnamese. He needed to respond. He authorized air strikes on military bases along the North Vietnamese coastline.

US involvement in the war grew. Johnson continued sending troops. By 1965, more than 50,000 US soldiers were serving in Vietnam.

THINK ABOUT IT

How was communism different from the US model of government? Why might the United States not want to support communism? What other countries did the United States support during the Cold War?

COMMUNISM VS. CAPITALISM

The communist system supports the idea of economic equality for all. To achieve this, the government controls all land, businesses, and resources. Private ownership is not allowed. The government distributes the wealth equally among the people. The United States uses a capitalist system. Land and businesses are privately owned. In theory, the wealthy, middle class, and poor get the wealth they earn.

Tonkin Incident Prompts Johnson to Military Action

On August 2, 1964, the US Navy destroyer *Maddox* was in the Gulf of Tonkin. It was patrolling international waters off the coast of North Vietnam. North Vietnam sent torpedo boats to attack the destroyer. Johnson warned the North Vietnamese against a similar assault. But two days later, on August 4, Johnson received reports of another attack. This time, two destroyers, the *Maddox* and the *C. Turner Joy,* had reportedly been attacked.

Johnson was under pressure from Congress and the public. They wanted the United States to do more to help resist Communists in Vietnam. Johnson quickly authorized air strikes against North Vietnam. He then took the incident to Congress. Johnson accused the North Vietnamese of committing "open aggression on the high seas." He called on Congress for the

The USS *Maddox* was attacked by the North Vietnamese in the Gulf of Tonkin.

The C. Turner Joy is now a ship museum in Bremerton, Washington.

power to use military action. They acted quickly. On August 7, the Gulf of Tonkin Resolution was passed unanimously in the House of Representatives. It had only two votes against it in the Senate.

The Gulf of Tonkin Resolution gave Johnson the power "to take all necessary steps, including the use of armed force." It was not an official declaration of war. But it was treated as such. In February 1965, the United States began bombings in North Vietnam.

THINK ABOUT IT

Research the Gulf of Tonkin Resolution to find out who voted against it. What reasons might they have had?

40

Time, in minutes, it took for the Gulf of Tonkin Resolution to pass through Congress.

- President Johnson received reports of North Vietnamese attacks on US destroyers in the Gulf of Tonkin on August 2 and 4, 1964.
- The Gulf of Tonkin Resolution was approved on August 7, 1964.
- Johnson used the Gulf of Tonkin Resolution to take greater action in Vietnam.

5

Unique Tactics and Technologies Used in Vietnam

During the Vietnam War, helicopters played an important role. In past wars, they had very limited use. But in Vietnam, the US Army began using them for military operations. Helicopters were used for observation and command functions. They were also used to carry soldiers into combat.

Helicopters changed the way wars were fought. The United States called their strategy "air mobility." It had never been used before. In the past, ground forces had been limited in their speed. Soldiers could advance only as far as their feet would take them. They were often blocked by rivers or mountains. Helicopters allowed the army to quickly drop soldiers directly into battle. Troops could be dropped in to support those already fighting. Or they could be placed at the enemy's rear to attack from both sides and cut off

Helicopters in Vietnam

20
Number of different types of helicopters used in the Vietnam War.

- Helicopters gave the US Army the ability to transport soldiers, weapons, and supplies quickly across Vietnam.
- The NLF was also known as the Viet Cong.
- Smaller, local Viet Cong groups used guerrilla warfare against US troops.

retreat. Helicopters were also used to transport wounded soldiers.

To combat the US forces, the Viet Cong used unique tactics. Also known as the National Liberation Front for South Vietnam (NLF), they had a central office and full-time soldiers. They carried out smaller attacks and were not as well trained as the North Vietnamese Army. They mostly took part in guerrilla warfare.

Guerrilla tactics included small ambushes, raids, sabotage, and hit-and-run strategies. The troops

> The Viet Cong sometimes traveled by sampan, or small boat.

set booby traps and land mines in the jungles and along roads. They planted bombs in towns where US troops were located. In combat, they used a tactic called "hanging onto the belts." They stayed as close to US troops as they could. This way, the Americans could not use air strikes without the risk of harming their own troops.

US Sustains Assault on North Vietnam

The Ho Chi Minh Trail connected North and South Vietnam. North Vietnam used it to send the Viet Cong supplies and troops. It passed through the countries of Laos and Cambodia. To disrupt the route, the United States targeted points along the trail. The first of these campaigns was Operation Barrel Roll. It began on December 14, 1964. Operation Steel Tiger came in April 1965. Operation Tiger Hound came that December.

President Johnson wanted to do more than just block the enemy's supply routes. The United States would use intense bombing. The plan was to destroy the Communists' will to fight. Such attacks would upset North Vietnam's ability to produce and transport supplies.

Operation Rolling Thunder was launched on March 2, 1965. At first, it targeted only the southern portion of North Vietnam. Over time, the

US paratroopers seeking Viet Cong snipers near Ben Cat, South Vietnam

643,000

Amount, in tons (583,320 metric tons), of bombs dropped on North Vietnam in Operation Rolling Thunder.

- In 1964, the United States began bombing the Ho Chi Minh Trail to disrupt supply routes.
- Operation Rolling Thunder launched on March 2, 1965.
- Some cities and important borders were off-limits to bombing attacks.
- North Vietnam used an air defense system.

UNCONVENTIONAL WEAPONS

The jungles of the Ho Chi Minh Trail were thick with plant life. This made it hard for US troops to monitor the enemy's movements. Agent Orange was an herbicide. US troops would spray it over the jungle. It would reveal the Viet Cong's hiding places. It also destroyed the crops the Viet Cong used for food. US troops used napalm bombs to destroy forests. The chemical mixture burned rapidly. One bomb could destroy 2,500 square yards (2,090 sq m) of jungle.

targeted areas rose northward. By mid-1966, targets spread throughout most of North Vietnam. Only the cities of Hanoi and Haiphong and a 10-mile (16-km) buffer zone bordering China were off-limits to attack.

With Operation Rolling Thunder under way, Johnson sent in the first ground forces. They were meant to defend the air bases. But they soon found themselves in active combat with the Viet Cong. North Vietnam sent more support to the Viet Cong. So Johnson sent more US troops.

North Vietnam had aid from China and the Soviet Union. With their help, North Vietnam built an air defense system. It shot down hundreds of US planes. Many of the pilots and systems operators were taken as prisoners of war.

Viet Cong Go Underground

In December 1965, Ho Chi Minh called for a change in military strategy. His army would no longer engage directly with US troops. They would use guerrilla warfare. This, along with their Soviet and Chinese weapons, would give them an edge in battle.

Now, it was even more important for the Viet Cong to hide their bases. In the jungle, they could use the forest as cover to hide from US air attacks. But near cities, there was less protection. Their solution was to move underground. Networks of underground tunnels gave the Viet Cong a place to hide. They also used the tunnels to move troops and supplies.

The tunnels allowed the Viet Cong to watch what the enemy was

Viet Cong guerrillas in a jungle clearing

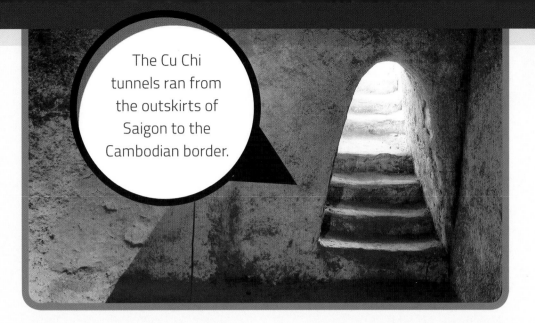

The Cu Chi tunnels ran from the outskirts of Saigon to the Cambodian border.

doing without them knowing. Tunnels crisscrossed the country. US troops occupied the ground above. But the Viet Cong were underneath. They were planning and launching attacks.

155

Combined length, in miles (250 km), of the Cu Chi tunnels.

- Ho Chi Minh's army adopted guerrilla tactics for the entire army in 1965.
- Underground tunnels allowed Viet Cong to evade detection.
- Soldiers trained as tunnel rats scouted for booby traps.

One of the largest tunnel networks was located underneath the Cu Chi district, northwest of Saigon. These tunnels linked soldiers as far away as the Cambodian border. The South Vietnamese and Americans trained soldiers to be tunnel rats. They scouted the tunnels and told troops above about booby traps.

LIVING UNDERGROUND

In some places, entire villages lived in underground shelters. The shelters had all the things people needed to survive, including kitchens, weapons factories, and hospitals. Some even had places for villages to gather, such as theaters and music halls.

North Vietnam Launches the Tet Offensive

The United States was dropping bombs and chasing down the enemy. But North Vietnamese General Vo Nguyen Giap was preparing an attack of his own. Secrecy was key to his plan. The US Army and South Vietnam were well armed. And they were winning on the battlefield. So a surprise attack was needed. Giap hoped the attack would inspire an uprising in the South Vietnamese. He believed a strong attack could divide the alliance between South Vietnam and the United States.

January 29, 1968, marked the celebration of the lunar New Year, Tet. It was Vietnam's most important holiday. Each year during this holiday, both sides observed a ceasefire. This way, everyone could celebrate the holiday. The South Vietnamese let

most of their troops go home. Just as the celebration and fireworks were ending, the North Vietnamese and Viet Cong attacked.

More than 100 cities, villages, and US bases were attacked at the same time. US Army leaders were stunned. They thought North Vietnam was struggling in the war. But all across

Vo Nguyen Giap was responsible for planning the Tet Offensive.

18

64

Number of district capitals attacked in the Tet Offensive.

- The Tet Offensive was launched on January 31, 1968.
- South Vietnam and the US Army were surprised by the attack.
- The North Vietnamese and Viet Cong had heavy casualties.
- After the attack, Americans wanted to scale back US involvement in the war.

HUE MASSACRE

The heaviest fighting of the Tet Offensive took place in the city of Hue. The battle raged for nearly a month. When the fighting ceased, US soldiers and South Vietnamese discovered a massacre. After seizing the city, the North Vietnamese army had done house-to-house searches of Hue. They captured and killed anyone linked to US or South Vietnamese forces. More than 2,800 citizens were buried in mass graves. Another 3,000 were missing.

the country, reports of attacks rolled in. It had taken the North Vietnamese and Viet Cong months to move troops and weapons into position. But the United States had failed to see the assault coming.

The 70,000 North Vietnamese and the Viet Cong attacked fiercely. They captured a radio station. They also blew a hole through a wall in the US embassy in Saigon. The attack was successful at first. But Giap's forces were spread too thin. They took heavy casualties. US and South Vietnamese forces pushed back

the Communist fighters. They put a quick end to most of the attacks. For every US and South Vietnamese soldier killed, the North Vietnamese lost more than 10. It was a major North Vietnamese military defeat.

President Johnson had promised the war's end was in sight. This large-scale assault had people at home thinking twice about continuing the war. Many Americans began withdrawing their support of the war effort. In the end, this made the Tet Offensive a political victory for North Vietnam.

Antiwar Movement Grows in the United States

Antiwar protests in the United States started small. They took place mainly on college campuses. Protesters opposed US involvement in Vietnam. They challenged the idea that a communist Vietnam posed a risk to US security. They also criticized Johnson for supporting the South Vietnamese government.

At first, protesters were in the minority. But by 1967, the antiwar movement had gained more support. Johnson had sent nearly 500,000 soldiers to Vietnam. The war was costing the United States $25 billion per year. And each day, US soldiers were being killed or wounded.

On October 21, 1967, an antiwar demonstration took place in Washington, DC. Approximately 100,000 protesters met outside the Lincoln Memorial. Later, approximately 30,000 marched on the Pentagon. Nearly 700 protesters were arrested as soldiers and US marshals blocked the building.

Johnson did not run for reelection in 1968. Richard Nixon took office in January 1969. He promised to restore law and order. He dismissed the protesters. He called them

Antiwar demonstrators in Washington, DC, protested against the Vietnam War.

In the draft lottery, all birthdates were put into a draw. The first one picked was given the number one.

a "vocal minority." Most Americans, the "silent majority," Nixon believed, supported the war.

For some time, young men had been called into service without volunteering. They were drafted. But on December 1, 1969, Nixon put the US draft lottery in place. All men aged 18 to 26 could be called upon to join the war effort. Men were then called into service based on their birthdates.

Many of those called to service opposed the war. Some were willing to serve. But they only wanted noncombat or public service jobs. Others dodged the draft. They faked

medical conditions and psychological problems, or they fled to Canada. They risked harsh jail sentences if caught.

18

Age at which young men become eligible for the draft.

- On October 21, 1967, a huge antiwar protest took place in Washington, DC.
- In 1968, Johnson decided not to seek reelection.
- Richard Nixon became president in January 1969.
- The US draft lottery was put in place in December of that year.

THINK ABOUT IT

Americans were divided in their opinions about US involvement in the Vietnam War. What are some reasons they opposed the war? What are some reasons they supported the war? What do you think the United States should have done in Vietnam?

21

10

Saigon Falls to the North Vietnamese

Nixon had an unpopular war on his hands. He adopted a new policy on the war in Vietnam. The United States would train and equip the South Vietnamese to fight on their own. Over time, US troops would withdraw from combat. Beginning in July 1969, the US Army began to remove its forces from Vietnam. More soldiers were going home than were being sent to Vietnam.

On March 29, 1973, the last US ground forces left Vietnam. By mid-1973, Congress passed a law that made it illegal for the president to spend money on US military operations in Indochina. The United States began reducing other military aid in South Vietnam. Without US support, South Vietnam had a hard time keeping its attackers at bay. The North Vietnamese made their way south. They claimed

US soldiers leaving Vietnam on March 29, 1973

Gerald Ford became US president after Nixon resigned.

new territory. They had their eyes set on Saigon, the South Vietnamese capital.

On August 9, 1974, US vice president Gerald Ford took office as the US president. As the North Vietnamese advanced south, Ford asked Congress to provide military aid to the South. Congress did not believe the South could win the war. They did provide some aid. But it was mostly used to remove Americans and some South Vietnamese from Saigon. Still, many South Vietnamese were left behind. Hundreds of thousands of South Vietnamese boarded boats. They attempted to flee the new regime.

Saigon fell on April 30, 1975. The South Vietnamese government had no option but to surrender. Saigon was renamed Ho Chi Minh City. Vietnam was reunited under a communist government.

20
Number of years the Vietnam War lasted.

- The last US troops were removed from Vietnam in 1973.
- The Vietnam War ended on April 30, 1975.
- Vietnam was united as a communist country.

23

As Vietnam Recovers, Refugees Flee

Military losses for the Vietnamese were high. In South Vietnam, 224,000 soldiers were killed and one million wounded. For North Vietnam and the Viet Cong, there were more than one million dead and 600,000 wounded. Approximately two million civilians lost their lives during the war as well.

Those who survived the war were left to pick up the pieces of their country. Bombing and ground warfare had destroyed

DEATH AND DESTRUCTION

Vietnam's landscape was devastated. Most of the fighting took place in South Vietnam. But the United States dropped bombs throughout Indochina. Agent Orange and napalm burns ruined the jungles. Agent Orange destroyed 4.5 million acres (1.8 million hectares) of land alone. It also killed or injured thousands of people. Many Vietnamese and US veterans still suffer from cancers and other illnesses thought to be caused by the chemical.

3.8 million

Number of North and South Vietnamese casualties of the war.

- Cities, villages, roads, and forests were destroyed by warfare.
- South Vietnamese who fought or aided the Americans risked punishment.
- South Vietnamese fled their country for North America, Europe, and Australia.

cities, villages, and forests. Roads had been destroyed as well. This destruction helped cut off supply routes during the war. But with the war over, it made it more difficult to reach civilians and rebuild. The country was littered with unexploded mines. Anyone who came upon these mines risked serious injury or death.

Many people living in South Vietnam were not happy with the war's outcome. Those who fought against the North risked punishment by the new regime. Anyone known to have aided the Americans, even entire villages, could be targeted for revenge. Approximately 65,000 Vietnamese were executed after the war. Another million were sent to prison camps.

Knowing they would be made to suffer, approximately 1.5 million South Vietnamese fled. But under the new government, leaving the country was illegal. They packed onto fishing boats and other vessels. A lot of these boats were

One of the few ways the Vietnamese could get out of the country was by boat.

unsafe for this kind of travel. Many refugees drowned in their attempts to leave. Those who made it out resettled in the United States, Great Britain, France, Australia, and Canada. For them, the war meant having to leave their homes. For those who stayed, it meant living in a new communist Vietnam.

Vietnam War Considered a US Loss

The Vietnam War was the first foreign war in which the United States failed to achieve its goals. It entered the conflict to prevent the spread of communism. But South Vietnam fell to the communist regime in the end.

The United States had spent approximately $200 billion trying to win. The cost of the war hurt the US economy for years to come. As a result, the United States became more wary of taking part in foreign wars.

Soldiers wait to return home to the United States.

In past wars, when soldiers returned home, they were greeted as heroes. But Vietnam veterans faced a poor response. Antiwar protesters did not think kindly of the soldiers. Even the war's supporters did not welcome soldiers home. The war and its outcome were unpopular with many Americans.

Still, a memorial was built in Washington, DC. The Vietnam Veterans Memorial was dedicated on November 13, 1982. The black

TIS P CHALLBERG · MICHAEL T BOAT · BARRETT C BROWN · ALBERT J CARRIER III
USHMAN · LAWRENCE R DETWILER Jr · MICHAEL J DUGAS · EDMUND FURMAN
ENNIS A GATTI · JOHN M HILL · LAWRENCE R GOODMAN Jr · MICHAEL J GRECU
RT F HEMP · LUIS MARTINEZ GONSALEZ · JOHN L HURD · ARTHUR H JOHNSON
AR · PETER A KIDD · MOSES I KUAHIWINUI Jr · ADREN A LEE · ROBERT D LINGLE
H LOVE · DOMINICK J MADONNA · ANTHONY V MIONE · STEPHEN D MOORE
ES E McWHORTER · JEFFREY C PETERSON · ROY K PETERSON · DERWIN B PITTS
N · ERIC D SALTZ · THOMAS R SAYERS · WILLIAM R SPEI   ARRELL D TAYLOR
IN T WALANGITANG · PETER LOPEZ · WILLIAM J ZELTNER   M C ADAMS
ES A WINGERT · TOMMY G ELLIOTT · W''LIAM W
V HALL · DENNIS C HUCKABY · HAYW
INETH D JOHNSON · JOE W NORWO
ER M MORALES · FREDERICK C
NGER · JIMMY JOE TENORIC
AMES N STEEN · WILLIA
IMMY M DOLAN · DAN
S L HENRY · WILLIA
JESUS DIEZ NIET
F ROSADO-BC
D A ANDERSC
BARRY B CO.
GENTRY · E
ES · DIXO!
IAEL G McG
V · ROBERT.
ES STIN
ON C
RLIN J C
ROGE!
VERLON
N R PEI
N RIV

· KENNETH A MEYER · TH
· JOHN E CARLSON · FREEM
· ROBERT F DALEY · THOMAS R POU
· JACK HARRIS Jr · JOHN J K/
· LARRY G MOOTHART · JOH
· KENNETH W PEASE · ARTHUR C FAIRCLO
· ALFRED G SAPP Sr · ROBERT E
· THEODORE W WEBB · JAM
JERRY E BARKER · RONALD B BISHOP · K
· EDDIE N CORSINO · DALE J CRIT
· DENNIS W FERGUSON · WIL
· WILLIAM C JOY · DONALD L
RICKY LEE MEEKS · DANA W MITCHE
AM T McNAIR · RICHARD E PEARSO
EODORE V SKILES · SCOTT P SMI
M TURNER · WILLIAM H WAI
· THOMAS E YOUNG · SCOTT
NY C CRAVENS · BRYAN J DEN
ANDALL L KRUEGER · ROBERT\
· JOHNNIE R MILLER · JERRY D
HN W TRACY · CORDIS R WH
MARTIN B DYER Jr · MONTY J.
· BERNARD J HENRY · JO
SAUNDERS · J LYNN STENHO!
· LELAND A BAILEY · WILLIAM C
LLIAM V FLYNN · ROBERT E LAVEN
E W SIMMERS Jr · WILFREDO B AN
· GROVER BOWEN · GREGORIC
· STEVEN V ELTING · JOE A
GG W HEIDRICH · JAMES W JACKSON
· THOMAS A LEICHLEITER · RAYMONI
HOMAS L LARSON · LEONEL MENDONC/
· BARRY K ALEXANDER · GLENN
· JOSHUA B STEWART · FRED E GOLD ·
· ERIC A LORD · JOHNNIE L
· CLINTON E MILLER · JAMES I YA

US architect Maya Lin designed the Vietnam Veterans Memorial.

granite monument is inscribed with more than 58,000 names. They are the dead and missing US servicemen and women of the Vietnam War. Over time, most Americans' feelings toward Vietnam veterans changed. They felt the soldiers deserved respect for having served their country in the armed forces.

2.6 million
Number of US men and women who served in Vietnam.

- The Vietnam War was the first foreign war the United States lost.
- The United States spent $200 billion on the Vietnam War.
- Vietnam veterans were not celebrated as heroes when they returned.
- The Vietnam War Memorial honors more than 58,000 dead and missing US servicemen and women.

12 Key Dates

March 12, 1947
US president Harry S. Truman announces the Truman Doctrine, promising US aid to countries threatened by communism.

July 21, 1954
The Geneva Accords divide Vietnam into two countries.

August 2, 1964
North Vietnam attacks the US destroyer *Maddox* in the Gulf of Tonkin.

August 4, 1964
President Lyndon B. Johnson receives reports of a North Vietnamese attack on two destroyers, the *Maddox* and the *C. Turner Joy.*

August 7, 1964
Congress approves the Gulf of Tonkin Resolution.

March 2, 1965
The US Army launches Operation Rolling Thunder.

October 21, 1967
Approximately 100,000 people take part in an antiwar protest in Washington, DC.

January 31, 1968
The Viet Cong and North Vietnamese launch the Tet Offensive.

December 1, 1969
Nixon puts the US draft lottery into effect.

March 29, 1973
The last US ground forces leave Vietnam.

April 30, 1975
Saigon falls to North Vietnam.

November 13, 1982
The Vietnam Veterans Memorial is dedicated.

Glossary

Allies
A group of countries that fought together in World War II and included the United States, Great Britain, China, and the Soviet Union.

arsenal
A weapons supply.

ceasefire
An agreement to temporarily stop fighting.

communist
A supporter of a political system where the government owns and controls property and wealth.

guerrilla
A person who takes part in small attacks or acts of terrorism, often as a member of an independent military unit.

herbicide
A chemical that kills plants.

intelligence
Information about the enemy.

menial
Something that lacks interest or dignity.

siege
A serious and lasting military attack.

For More Information

Books

Caputo, Phillip. *10,000 Days of Thunder: A History of the Vietnam War.* New York: Atheneum Books for Young Readers, 2011.

Meyers, Walter Dean. *Patrol: An American Soldier in Vietnam.* New York: Harper Collins, 2005.

Murray, Stuart A. P. *DK Eyewitness Books: Vietnam War.* New York: DK Children, 2005.

Visit 12StoryLibrary.com

Scan the code or use your school's login at **12StoryLibrary.com** for recent updates about this topic and a full digital version of this book. Enjoy free access to:

- Digital ebook
- Breaking news updates
- Live content feeds
- Videos, interactive maps, and graphics
- Additional web resources

Note to educators: Visit 12StoryLibrary.com/register to sign up for free premium website access. Enjoy live content plus a full digital version of every 12-Story Library book you own for every student at your school.

Index

About the Author

Jill Sherman lives and writes in Brooklyn, New York. She has written more than a dozen books for young readers. She enjoys researching new topics and is honored to share the important moments of the Vietnam War with readers.

READ MORE FROM 12-STORY LIBRARY

Every 12-Story Library book is available in many formats. For more information, visit 12StoryLibrary.com.